RUE
DU CHAT-
QUI-PÊCHE

RUE
DU CHAT-
QUI-PÊCHE

Young Explorers

AROUND
PARIS

Text by Daniela Celli

Illustrations by Laura Re

DEAR PARENTS

Traveling with children can be complicated and tiring,
BUT ALSO INCREDIBLY FUN AND EXTRAORDINARY.
And, in particular, visiting Paris with children can really
be an exciting experience. Without them, Pompidou would simply
be a wacky building that clashes with the surrounding architecture,
and many of you probably wouldn't laugh in front of the obelisk in
Place de la Concorde, imagining a skewer bitten by a giant.
And what excuse would you find to push the boats
of the Jardin des Tuileries with a stick?

THIS BOOK, A COLLECTION OF STORIES AND CURIOSITIES, WILL HELP YOU
TRAVEL TO PARIS WHILE ON YOUR SOFA OR IN REAL LIFE, ACCOMPANIED BY
AN EXCEPTIONAL GUIDE...

Inside you will find everything that I discovered while traveling with
my children through *rues* and *places*, including that pinch of magic
that the *Ville-Lumière* gives to those who admire it in wonderment
and that I hope will reach you, too.

To BG,
my jazz to the route to Oz.

Daniela Celli

BONJOUR, MY LITTLE FRIENDS!

Let me introduce myself: I am the *Chat Noir*, and it will be a real pleasure to take you around Paris with me. This *cité* is so full of curious places, funny stories, and sometimes even creepy tales that we surely won't get bored!

Did you know, for example, that GOATS are used in some grassy areas to cut the lawn instead of lawnmowers? And that *Montmartre* has a HEADLESS GHOST?

Alors, if you are eager to know more, we can start: I have prepared FOUR DIFFERENT ITINERARIES for you that will lead us to discover palaces and museums, squares, cathedrals, and alleys.

Each itinerary begins with a MAP, where you will find our planned STOPS. And don't worry if you get hungry: *bien sûr*, I thought about that, too!

And between one wonder and another there will even be time to play some games together... THE IMPORTANT THING IS TO ALWAYS KEEP YOUR EYES WIDE OPEN!

BON VOYAGE!

ITINERARIES

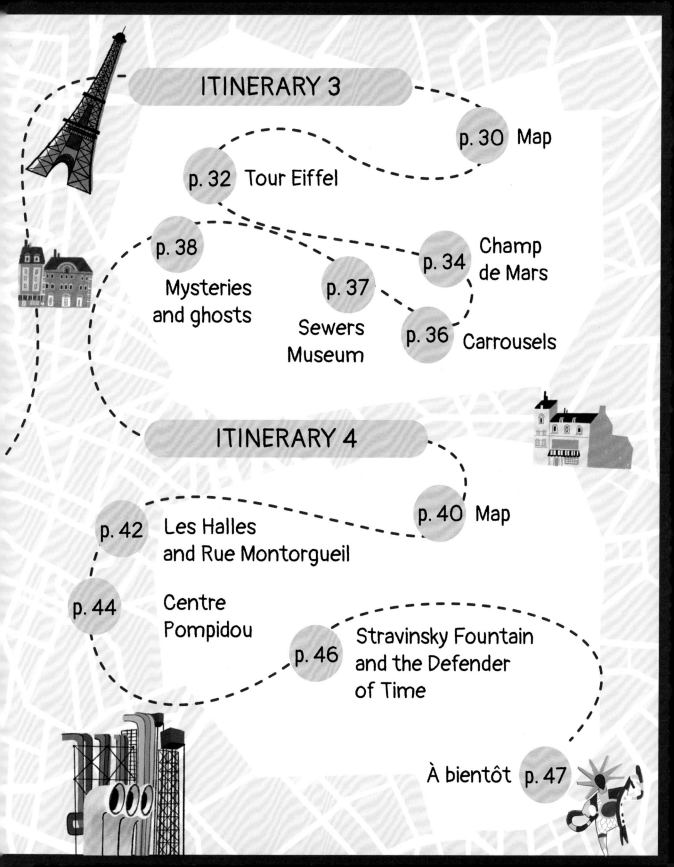

PARIS

*Bonjour, girls and boys,
and welcome to the City of Lights!*

5 ARC DE TRIOMPHE

4 CHAMPS-ÉLYSÉES

3 PLACE DE LA CONCORDE

RIVER SEINE

ITINERARY 1

I have prepared an itinerary that includes MUMMIES and STRANGE MONUMENTS, leading us to the discovery of three *arrondissements*.
WHAT ARE THEY?
Alors, try to imagine Paris as a large snail whose shell expands from the center outward. Each section is an *arrondissement*, or district. We start with number 1, which is where we are now, and by wandering around, we arrive at number 20.

JARDIN DES TUILERIES

2

LOUVRE 1

• La Ville-Lumière

At the time of the SUN KING, Louis XIV, electric lighting did not yet exist, so citizens were asked to keep lit candles in their windows. With the introduction of GAS LIGHTING, street lamps and lanterns appeared: by 1870, there were more than twenty thousand of them in the city. This is why Paris is nicknamed "THE CITY OF LIGHTS."

• Along the Seine

Paris was first settled and developed around the Seine, one of the most important rivers in France. There are 37 bridges in the city, each one with its own peculiarities.
Do you know, for example, which one is the oldest? The one called *Pont Neuf* (New Bridge). OBVIOUS, RIGHT?

THE LOUVRE

Et voilà, we are about to enter one of the largest museums in the world, with over 380,000 objects and works of art!

• A pyramid in the center of Paris?
Can you imagine a more spectacular entrance than this?
To enter the museum you have to go inside a pyramid made up
of 675 glass squares and 118 glass triangles!

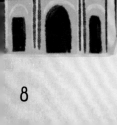

The building that houses the *Louvre Museum* was built on the site of a fortress from the Middle Ages that protected Paris from the VIKINGS, and it later became the PALACE OF THE KINGS.

Visiting it is like entering a time machine: You can walk among the mummies of ancient Egypt or alongside the statues of ancient Greece, or you can admire the works of the most important European painters.

The museum offers several itineraries for children; try, for example, the exciting TREASURE HUNT!

ALLEZ, THOUSANDS OF WONDERS ARE WAITING FOR US!

HERE ARE SOME UNMISSABLE
TREASURES OF THE MUSEUM:
LET'S GET TO KNOW THEM BETTER ...

• The adventures of the *Dame de Auxerre*

Before finding its home in the Louvre, this statue
from Crete, sculpted almost THREE thousand years
AGO, went through lots of adventures!
It was part of a theater show, became a hat rack, and
was abandoned in the street until an archaeologist
found it!

• *Bienvenue* in Egypt

With over 50,000 pieces, the collection dedicated
to ancient Egypt is the second most important
in the world, after that of the Egyptian Museum
in Cairo, and it will allow you to discover the secrets of an
extraordinary people!

Did you know, for example, that the Egyptians
mummified bodies so that they would be
preserved forever in the KINGDOM OF
THE DEAD? The technique involved
the extraction of the internal
organs and a long immersion
in salted water. The body was
then covered with oils and
wrapped in bandages to end
up in a...SARCOPHAGUS!

• On the run with the diamond

The *Régent* is one of the largest diamonds in the world. Before being exhibited in the *Louvre* it shone on the crown of a king and on the hilt of NAPOLEON's sword.

• All Crazy for the Mona Lisa

Leonardo da Vinci's famous painting is now well protected from potential theft. But who would dare to steal the legendary *Mona Lisa*? Well, one night in 1911, the painting disappeared and was found two years later in Florence. The thief was the Italian VINCENZO PERUGGIA, who had succeeded in the act by pretending to be a museum worker!

• Venus the heartbreaker

Found by chance by a Greek farmer in 1820, the famous *Venus de Milo* was literally in pieces: The bust didn't have arms, and the legs were also missing but were later found after digging nearby.

DESPITE ITS STATE, IT WAS STILL BEAUTIFUL, AND EVEN KING LOUIS XVIII WOULD SPEND HOURS AND HOURS CONTEMPLATING IT!

JARDIN DES TUILERIES

Welcome to the tile garden! Do you want to know why it has such an unusual name?

Queen Catherine de Medici had her new palace built here.
She wanted it to feature a beautiful garden, full of fountains and mazes, like the one at her Florence home, and for this reason she brought in an architect from Italy.

But at that time this area was occupied by the shops that made tiles for the roofs of all the houses, *les tuileries*.

THAT'S WHY IT STILL HAS THIS NAME TODAY!

• Let's play sailors!

WHAT DID YOU SAY...THAT THERE IS NO
SEA IN PARIS? *Meoww*, you are right, but
Alain and his small *bateaux* can help us!
These boats with colorful sails were built by him,
following a tradition that has been going on for
150 years!
GET ONE AND PUSH IT ACROSS THE LAKE WITH A STICK,
THEN THE WIND WILL DO THE REST!

Search and find
How about a game?
Look around and try to find:

12 pigeons

3 balls

3 bicycles

1 dog

...and my
little tail!

PLACE DE LA CONCORDE

Allez mes amis, just a few more steps and we are there!
Welcome to the Place de la Concorde!

Nowadays this name recalls peace and harmony, but it wasn't always this way. During the French Revolution, it was here where they placed the guillotine, a terrible machine used to cut off the heads of those sent to death; among them were KING LOUIS XVI, MARIE ANTOINETTE, and thousands more.

• Cleopatra's Needle

And now look over there. Isn't this long stone "skewer" magnificent?
It was built by Pharaoh RAMESSES II over 3,000 years ago, and it remained in Egypt until 1833, when it was offered to France as a gift. The obelisk is covered with hieroglyphics, and if you look at the base you will notice the drawings that show the machinery that was used for its transportation.

DO YOU THINK YOU COULD MOVE
THE WEIGHT OF 40 ELEPHANTS!

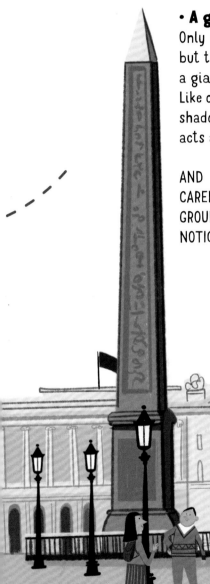

• A giant clock
Only a few know this, but the obelisk is also a giant sundial.
Like other sundials, its shadow on the square acts as a hand.

AND IF YOU LOOK CAREFULLY ON THE GROUND, YOU WILL ALSO NOTICE THE NUMBERS.

Do you want to build a sundial?

MATERIALS:
• a stick
• 12 pebbles
• a sunny day

INSTRUCTIONS:
Plant the stick upright in the ground. Wait for the top of the hour and mark the spot where the stick's shadow falls with a pebble. Do the same every hour until the sun sets. *Et voilà*, the next day, by observing the shadow cast by the stick, you will know what time it is!

AVENUE DES CHAMPS- ÉLYSÉES

See this beautiful tree-lined avenue that is over two miles long?
It is one of the most famous streets in the world! When strolling along,
you will see gardens, palaces, luxury shops, cinemas, and restaurants.
A true paradise!

BUT WAIT A SECOND! I FEEL A LITTLE HUNGRY...HOW ABOUT
A *CROQUE-MONSIEUR* BEFORE CARRYING ON?

• *Monsieur et Madame*
It is not known exactly why this grilled toast stuffed with ham, cheese,
and bechamel is called Croque-Monsieur ("*bite the gentleman*"), but I can
confirm that it is delicious! There is also a "female" version that
involves adding a fried egg!

ARC DE TRIOMPHE

After winning the famous Battle of Austerlitz, Emperor NAPOLEON BONAPARTE told his soldiers, "You will return to your homes only through arches of triumph!" That same year, the first stone of this famous monument was laid in Paris. It actually took a long time to finish—30 YEARS!

• A prodigious feat

A century after Napoleon, someone took his statement literally. To celebrate the end of the First World War, aviator *Charles Godefroy* flew his biplane straight through the Arc de Triomphe!

Bonjour, mes petits voyageurs!

RIVER SEINE

4 MUSÉE D'ORSAY

RUE DU CHAT-QUI-PÊCHE

2

5ᵉ Arr
RUE D
CHAT-QUI-PÊ

JARDIN DU LUXEMBOURG

3

18

ITINERARY 2

Today's adventure will take us for a walk on the river islands of Paris, where one of the most famous cathedrals in the world is located. Then we will continue our tour and discover some areas of the *Rive Gauche*, the left bank of the Seine, the river that divides the city in two.

1

NOTRE-DAME

Glacier depuis 1954

• City beaches

As soon as summer comes, large boats unload tons of sand on the riverbank, along with palm trees and lounge chairs, transforming part of the riverbank into real beaches! ISN'T IT *FANTASTIQUE*?

• A beautiful and useful gift

Among the numerous Parisian fountains, try to look for the *fontaines Wallace*.

They have been offering FREE DRINKING WATER for over 150 years. There are at least a hundred dark green fountains, decorated with marine snakes, caryatids, and dolphins.

Can you spot any on the map?

NOTRE-DAME AND THE CITY ISLANDS

We are on the *Île de la Cité*, an island in the heart of Paris!

What you see is *Notre-Dame*, the most famous GOTHIC CHURCH in the world. It's over 700 years old, but on a sad day in 2019, it was damaged by a fire that caused the spire and the roof to collapse.
It will take time before everything is back to the way it was!

• Creepy gutters

Can you see those monstrous figures? They are *gargouilles* (gargoyles) that drain out the water when it rains. In the past, however, it was also believed that they protected against evil.

• The great Emmanuel

There are 10 bells in *Notre-Dame*. The biggest, *Emmanuel*, weighs over 13 tons. That's the equivalent of 9 hippos!

• Delicious snacks

It's time to get a *goûter*! This is what you call a SNACK in French, and here is the perfect place: *Berthillon*, the oldest ice cream shop in Paris! Look for it on the map before deciding WHICH FLAVOR YOU WANT!

A TASTE OF TOPONYMY

Toponymy is the science that studies the names of places.

• Streets with no name

At one time in Paris, as in many other cities, the streets did not have names, and arranging to meet up was very complicated: *"ALORS,* SEE YOU TOMORROW IN THAT LITTLE ROAD ON THE LEFT BANK OF THE RIVER, AS WIDE AS SIX MEDIUM-SIZED DOGS, WHERE THERE IS THAT TAVERN WHOSE SIGN OUTSIDE SHOWS A CAT RUNNING AWAY..."
Fortunately, in 1728, things changed, and today each street has a name, written on a beautiful blue plaque.

• Rue du Chat-qui-Pêche

This is one of the narrowest streets in Paris. According to legend, it was given this name ("cat who fishes") because a cat lived there that was so skillful at fishing it needed just one paw to catch the fish.

FANCY A GAME?

Come up with a funny name for a street
and imagine the story behind it!

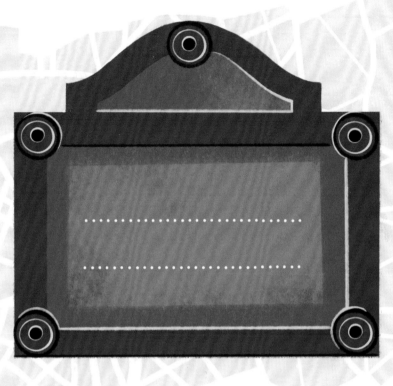

. . . .

. . . .

Some French words

- *Avenue*: main street or avenue
- *Ruelle*: small alley
- *Promenade*: a place to stroll
- *Quai*: riverside
- *Rue*: street
- *Place*: square
- *Montée*: sloping street

23

JARDIN DU LUXEMBOURG

The Luxembourg Garden is one of the largest and most elegant public parks in Paris, a green oasis where children can have fun feeding the ducks—*les canards*—pushing the boats in the *Grand Bassin*, or attending a show!

• Do you like *les marionnettes*?

Robert Desarthis loved them ever since he was a child. It was he who created the first PUPPET THEATER in France, which has been at the center of the park for almost a hundred years.

• The sisters of Lady Liberty

Everyone knows the famous Statue of Liberty: it is a symbol of New York City. But it was the French who gifted it to the United States! There are SIX COPIES in Paris, albeit a lot smaller, and one of them is right here.

DO YOU SEE IT?

Search and find
In the jardin there are 106 statues. Find the ones in the shape of...

• a lion   • an owl
• a deer   • a dolphin

MUSÉE D'ORSAY

Bienvenue au Musée!

It seems incredible, but where paintings, statues, and others works of art are now exhibited, there were once trains departing and arriving: The *Musée d'Orsay* was a train station! If you look carefully, you will easily see clues to its past: the names on the facade, the giant clocks, and the glass roof.

• En plein air
The largest collection of paintings by Impressionist and post-Impressionist artists like MONET and VAN GOGH, who loved to paint in the open air, is kept here.
Instead of reproducing what they saw, like in a photograph, the Impressionists let themselves be inspired by LIGHT and color, and stroke by stroke, they created their MASTERPIECES.

• Bizarre containers
Before 1841 when the American *John Goffe Rand* invented the tin tubes paint is kept in, paints were kept inside containers made out of...pig bladders. BLECH!

• Ours Blanc
This super-smooth statue, without a hair out of place, is *François Pompon*'s white bear, the symbol of the museum.

WHAT A CELEBRITY!

Let's discover a few secrets about three famous people from place we've visited!

• A passion for caricatures

(We met Monet at the Musée D'Orsay)

Famous Impressionist painter *Claude Monet* did not like going to school. To fight away boredom during lessons, he used to scribble in the margins of books: he drew garlands and fantastical decorations but also...his teachers, exaggerating their features.

THE SCIENCE TEACHER WOULD BECOME A SMALL MAN WITH A HUGE NOSE, AND THE FRENCH TEACHER WOULD END UP WITH A BIG WART!

• Quasimodo's "father"
(The bell ringer of Notre-Dame)
The great French writer *Victor Hugo* lived most of his life in Paris, where many of his novels are set.

HIS NOVEL *NOTRE-DAME DE PARIS* TELLS THE STORY OF QUASIMODO, THE HUNCHED BELL-RINGER WHO LIVES BEHIND THE SPIRES OF NOTRE-DAME.

• The wrongfully accused emperor
(We met Napoleon at the Arc de Triomphe)
A lot of nonsense circulates about *Napoleon Bonaparte*, king of Italy and emperor of France: It is said that he was very short, that he "stole" the *Mona Lisa* from Italy, and that he suffered from such a terribly upset stomach that he always kept a hand inside his vest.

IN REALITY NAPOLEON WAS 5 FOOT, THE *MONA LISA* WAS TAKEN TO FRANCE BY LEONARDO DA VINCI, AND HE KEPT HIS HAND INSIDE HIS VEST ONLY WHEN HE HAD A PORTRAIT MADE, AS WAS CUSTOMARY AT THE TIME!

Ready for *une nouvelle aventure?*

TOUR EIFFEL 1

3 CARROUSELS

4 SEWERS MUSEUM

2 CHAMP DE MARS

ITINERARY 3

Today we will climb to the top of the most famous symbol of Paris, we will play in a lovely park full of statues and fountains, and then we will explore underground, descending into mysterious, stinky...I mean, charming tunnels!

RIVER SEINE

• As strong as a...rooster

Once upon a time, France was inhabited by a people that the Romans called GAULS. The warriors wore helmets with two rooster wings carved on them, and today *le coq*, the rooster, is an emblem of France—it's even represented on sportswear!

• The fly boat

A fascinating way to visit the city is from the river, perhaps on a *bateau mouche*. Can you see it on the map? The idea of having tourists travel the Seine originated almost a century ago, when *Jean Bruel* bought a boat that he called THE OLD FLY.

THE TOUR EIFFEL

MEOWWW, sorry my friends, but even if I live in Paris it is always very *émotionel* being in front of one of the most loved monuments in the world—the Eiffel Tower. However, when Mr. Gustave Eiffel presented his project for the UNIVERSAL EXHIBITION, many criticized it by calling the tower a monstrous IRON ASPARAGUS.

• Ready in record time

Despite the difficulty of assembling 18,000 pieces of iron at dizzying heights, the project took only two years to complete!

On the day of the inauguration, March 31, 1889, Eiffel went up the 1,710 steps leading to the top, hoisted the French flag, and fired 21 cannon shots.

• Change in appearance

La Dame de Fer, as we French love calling it, hasn't always been brown.

Gustave Eiffel initially had it painted red, and later, it was bronze and yellow ocher, too.

• A sweet view

How about climbing to the top? The view is *stupéfiant*, and on the second floor is a bar that sells *macarons*, delicious pastries made of two meringues joined by a filling of different flavors and colors: strawberry pink, pistachio green, chocolate brown...and also pumpkin orange, my favorite!

1889

CHAMP DE MARS

In front of the *Tour Eiffel* is the *Champ de Mars*, another large public garden full of beautiful flower beds, ponds, and avenues to stroll, jog, or sit by for a picnic while admiring the Iron Lady. The garden was designed at the behest of Louis XV, who decided to have a military school built there, too. This is why it is called Champ de Mars, a tribute to Mars, the Roman god of war!

• War and peace

At the end of the park, a stone's throw from the military school, there is the WALL OF PEACE, a beautiful monument made of a long glass plate on which the word "peace" is written in 32 LANGUAGES. In French we say *paix*. Do you know how to say it in any other language?

• Flight tests

The *Montgolfier* brothers, the inventors of the hot air balloon, carried out some of their test flights right here.

THE FIRST AIR PASSENGERS WERE A SHEEP, A GOOSE, AND A ROOSTER!

Search and find
Things that fell from the balloon:

- a pair of glasses
- a baguette
- a book
- a toothbrush
- a baloon

35

CARROUSELS

No child can go to Paris without taking at least one ride on one of the many *carrousels*, the fairground rides with wooden horses.

The most spectacular is the one in front of the *Pont d'Iéna*. Where else could you enjoy a ride between a river and an iron tower?

• An idea from the past

In medieval fairgrounds, the galloping knight had to hit a puppet that rotated around an axis.

THAT'S WHERE THE IDEA CAME FROM!

• Not just horses

You can also ride on other animals on Parisian carousels, not just horses. At the *Jardin des Plantes* there are lions, turtles, and elephants, and at *La Villette* you can ride aboard aircraftand trains.

SEWERS MUSEUM

And now we go under! Under where? Underground!
At the *Musée des Egouts* you can explore underground and
discover all the secrets of a mechanism that is fundamental
for every city!

• The great stink

In the past, there were no sewers
and all waste water, noxious and
stinking, ended up in the streets!
Fortunately, today there is a
system of underground tunnels
that collect the waste and keep it
away from the city.

• Pay attention *aux rats!*

Rodents are known to be real
sewer lovers! Speaking of *rats*,
have you watched the film
Ratatouille? At the beginning
of his adventure, Rémy gets
lost here!

AND NOW TELL ME, ARE YOU BRAVE?
IF YOU ARE, THEN YOU CAN TURN THE PAGE...

MYSTERIES AND GHOSTS!

• The Phantom of the Opera

(Opéra Garnier, Place de l'Opéra IXᵉ arrondissement)

Since it was built, the Opéra Garnier, which is the most famous Parisian theater, has been the scene of numerous mysterious events, like noises coming from underground. The "culprit" was said to be hiding in the tunnels under the theater—the ghost of a masked pianist whose face was disfigured after a fire.

• The legend of the philosopher's stone

(Maison Nicholas Flamel, 51 rue de Montmorency, IIIᵉ arrondissement)

Have you ever heard of Nicholas Flamel and the philosopher's stone? It is said that this old man, who was an alchemist and also a bit of a magician, invented a stone capable of transforming metals into gold and also manufactured the elixir of life, a magical concoction that makes whoever drinks it immortal! According to legend the man hid the secret formula in his home.

IF YOU WANT TO TRY YOUR LUCK AND FIND IT, GO TO THE MARAIS!

• The headless ghost

(Fontaine du Square Suzanne-Buisson, Montmartre XVIIIe arrondissement)

When strolling through the neighborhood of *Montmartre*, you might come across a fountain topped by an unusual statue of a man holding his own severed head in his hands; it represents the first bishop of Paris and martyr *Saint Denis*.
ACCORDING TO LEGEND, AFTER HAVING BEEN BEHEADED, THE POOR MAN PICKED UP HIS HEAD, WASHED IT, AND KEPT WALKING FOR SIX MILES.

• Stations Fantômes

(Porte des Lilas-Cinema)

What secrets are hidden in the GHOST METRO STATIONS? They are actually called that because they were abandoned and are no longer in use. This does not detract from the charm of these mysterious places.

Can you believe that we've already gotten to the last *itinéraire* ?

LES HALLES

①

RUE MONTORGUEIL

②

CENTRE POMPIDOU

ITINERARY 4

Eh bien oui, when walking around Paris, time flies!
So, we better start since we have tons of fun things to see and do on the *rive Droite*! We'll find interesting signs on a delightful street, then go to one of the strangest museums in the world, and finally we will visit a certain character who...be patient!
EVERYTHING AT THE RIGHT TIME...

THE DEFENDER 4
OF TIME

3
STRAVINSKY
FOUNTAIN

• Ecological lawn mowers
To mow the green spaces alongside the boulevards, a system called ECO-PASTURE has recently been adopted.
Instead of lawnmowers, you can rent a goat or a ram that is happy to work...while eating.

• Empty the attic!
If you continue to walk around the *arrondissements*, you might bump into a *vide-grenier*, the famous "attic-emptying" market. Adults and children can get rid of what they don't use anymore, instead of leaving it "to the fleas"! If you don't know this already, the *marché aux puces*, typical of Paris, are markets where second-hand goods are sold.

LES HALLES
AND RUE MONTORGUEIL

Welcome to the oldest AND newest market in town!

Oh no, *mes amis,* I'm not crazy. Where today there is a brand new shopping mall covered by a glass roof, in the past was a large area where traders came to sell their goods: *Les Halles* was the first Parisian market.

• An appetizer to eat...slowly!

For almost two centuries, the restaurant *L'Escargot Montorgueil* has been offering its guests a typical French dish: snails! *Escargots* are usually served with a special two-hooked fork that you need to extract the cooked snails from their shells!

Are you suddenly really hungry for grey mullet, too?
Luckily we are in the right neighborhood! *Rue Montorgueil* hosts fruit and vegetable stalls, cheese shops, pastry shops, and *très délicieux restaurants*.

• Sweets worthy of a king

Stohrer, the oldest patisserie in Paris, was founded in 1730 by the chief *pâtissier* of the king of Poland, whose daughter married Louis XV. The chef followed her to the palace of *Versailles*, where he came up with many delicacies, including the famous rum baba. According to legend, the clever pastry chef decided to soften the baba with liquor because the girl's father had no teeth!

Search and find
Some of the signs indicate what is sold inside the magasin (store). Can you find the signs of the following stores?

- L'Escargot Montorgueil
- La Fermette cheese shop
- Le Palais du Fruit
- Café Montorgueil

CENTRE POMPIDOU

Welcome to the *Centre Pompidou*, the cultural center that houses one of the greatest collections of modern and contemporary art from around the world. Does it look like a giant alien ship to you?

When it was built in 1977 not everyone appreciated its eccentric structure. On the external walls you can clearly see everything that is usually hidden inside buildings: pipes, elevators, escalators, and electrical conduits, everything in its own color!

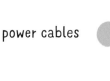

elevators and escalators ●

power cables ●

air vents ●

• Neverending masterpieces

The *Beaubourg*, as we Parisians love to call it, hosts over 100,000 works of art created in the last 100 years: Picasso, Chagall, Magritte, and Kandinsky are just some of the great artists in the museum.

HAVE YOU EVER SEEN ANY OF THEIR PAINTINGS?

• Learn by playing

The *Galerie de Enfants* is an area entirely dedicated to child artists. Here you can play, touch works of art, experiment, and build your own masterpieces!

DO YOU LIKE MY SELF-PORTRAIT? WOULD YOU LIKE TO TRY AND MAKE YOURS?

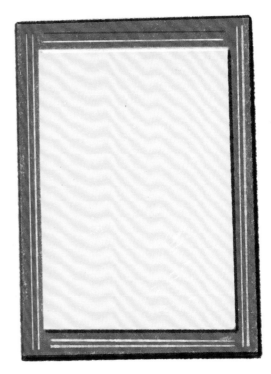

STRAVINSKY FOUNTAIN AND THE DEFENDER OF TIME

What a fountain! To me it's as beautiful as a thousand sardines! The sprinkling water coming out of those bizarre figures is so shiny! Some of them even move! Better stay back...

UM, I REALLY DO NOT LIKE GETTING WET!

• The Stravinsky Fountain

It is a tribute to the great musician and composer *Igor Stravinsky*. The sixteen aluminum figures that make up the fountain have shapes inspired by his works, and they dance like they are in a ballet.

• Like in a fairy tale

The animal with strange wings and a crown of golden feathers is "the Firebird," a character from *Stravinsky's* ballet of the same name.

The Russian fairy tale that inspired it tells of a prince in love, an evil magician capable of turning people into stone, and a bird with magical feathers!

• The Defender of Time

Meow, I would like to take you to see one last thing: an extraordinary clock!

It is located on the facade of a building in *Rue Bernard de Clairvaux*, and it features moving figures.

At the stroke of every hour, the man with the sword and the shield fights against one or all of three animals: a bird, a dragon, and a crab that all create a cacophony of sounds.

And do you know who he is? THE DEFENDER OF TIME.

À BIENTÔT

It's time to say goodbye...
Remember this, children: Time is a precious thing, and the time spent discovering the world is never wasted time!

Word of the Chat Noir

LAURA RE

Born in Rome, Laura attended the Rome School of Comics, after which she collaborated with animation studios as a character designer, concept artist, and illustrator. After attending the International School of Illustration in Sàrmede, Italy, she moved to Milan to attend Mimaster's Master in Illustration. Here she deepened her knowledge of the publishing sector and the world of illustration for children.

Graphic layout: Valentina Figus

DANIELA CELLI

Born in Florence in 1977, Daniela studied piano at the Luigi Cherubini Conservatory, after which she moved to New York and began studying criminology. In 1997, she returned to Italy, graduated in law, and obtained a diploma from the Academy of Dramatic Arts. Always passionate about travel, since 2008 she has been blogging about adventures with her family around the world.

WHITE STAR KIDS

White Star Kids™ is a trademark of White Star s.r.l.

© 2022 White Star s.r.l.
Piazzale Luigi Cadorna, 6
20123 Milan, Italy
www.whitestar.it

Translation: Inga Sempel
Editing: Michele Suchomel-Casey

Printing, December 2023

ISBN 978-88-544-1866-0
 3 4 5 6   27 26 25 24 23

Printed and manufactured in China
by Guangzhou XY Printing Co., Ltd.

The *Chat Noir* has been living in Paris since 1881. They say that a man named Salis saw him wandering around the alleys by his bar and decided to call him by this name; the cat became so famous that he was featured in magazines and on posters. He loves fried fish and ghost stories, and he knows every secret in the city!